Wend,
"Summer in Canada 2005"
Haste ye back!
Love, Wendy.

NOVA SCOTIA

PHOTOGRAPHS BY

Paul Nicholson

NIMBUS
PUBLISHING

Nimbus Publishing Limited
PO Box 9166
Halifax, NS   B3K 5M8
(902) 455-4286

Printed and bound in Singapore
Design: Troy Cole – Envision Graphic Design

Paul Nicholson's photographs, including those in this publication, can
be viewed and purchased at www.novascotiaphotos.com.

Library and Archives Canada Cataloguing in Publication

    Nicholson, Paul (Paul D.)
    Nova Scotia / Paul Nicholson.

    ISBN 1-55109-528-9

1. Nova Scotia—Pictorial works. I. Title.

FC2312.N52 2005   971.6'05'0222   C2005-900359-6

We acknowledge the financial support of the Government of Canada
through the Book Publishing Industry Development Program (BPIDP)
and the Canada Council for our publishing activities.

TITLE PAGE ⌐ *Tuna fishing near Betty's Island, off the coast of Prospect.*

DEDICATION

*T*his book is dedicated to my
daughters, Amy and Hannah.

⌐ Paul Nicholson

A sun muted by fog creates a dreamy light over Queensland Beach, near Hubbards.

BELOW — *An abandoned house in Bayside, a small community near Halifax, perfectly complements this still winter scene.*

From the lush farms of the Annapolis Valley to the rocky wilderness of the Cape Breton Highlands, Nova Scotia is celebrated for its picture-perfect landscapes and breathtaking scenery. Here, colourful fishing villages cling to steep rocks; South Shore beaches stretch for miles; the magnificent Fundy tides leave intricate patterns in exposed red mud. Even Nova Scotia's urban scenes are more landscape than cityscape. Consider, for example, picturesque Halifax buildings alight underneath the star-shaped Citadel, or a bridge spanning the deep natural harbour on a foggy winter morning. As authentic and unmistakably Nova Scotian as many of the province's icons are, any Bluenose will tell you that it's the land itself that is the root of Nova Scotia's character. Anyone who has hiked the Cabot Trail or to Cape Split's dramatic look-off would say the same.

Small wonder, then, that settlers from all over the world have made this place their home, joining the Mi'kmaq—who have lived here for thousands of years—in relishing the bounty of the area's sea, forests, and rivers. In 1605 the first French settlers arrived, calling the region Acadia. A peaceful agricultural people who forged strong alliances with the Mi'kmaq, the Acadians claimed farmland from the sea by building dykes, creating incredibly rich soil and becoming a prosperous society.

But the British also recognized the virtues of Nova Scotia, and fought furiously with the French for a century and a half, eventually claiming the land as their own. They deported the Acadians and imported New England Planters. When some beleaguered Acadians began returning to Nova Scotia, they found their homes and farms occupied—or destroyed. Today, Acadian communities like Chéticamp and Ste.-Anne are predominantly French speaking, and there are numerous initiatives underway to preserve and celebrate Acadian traditions. There are also thriving Mi'kmaw communities in the province, such as those at Bear River and at Membertou in Sydney; despite the turbulence created by the early settlers, native culture has persevered, and remains an essential part of Nova Scotia's cultural roots.

As Nova Scotia developed, it continued to attract other distinct groups: Germans, Loyalists (including a large number of black Loyalists), Scots, Irish, Welsh, and numerous others arrived—and continue to arrive—in Nova Scotia. This influx of immigrants, a defining element of this place, has resulted in a rich assortment of cultural influences. From coast to coast, the province's robust musical heritage—from

bluegrass and country to celtic—and its delectable culinary traditions, inspired from bountiful harvests of ocean and land, live on in the daily life and joyous celebrations of its people.

Perhaps most profoundly, it is Nova Scotia's diverse physical landscape which best complements its vibrant cultural fabric. Hence, Kejimkujik National Park's plentiful fresh-water lakes and ancient hemlock forests evoke days of Mi'kmaw travel by canoe and portage; Lunenburg's classic harbour, a UNESCO World Heritage Site, retains all the flavour of the Age of Sail; the rich, fertile fields and orchards of the Annapolis Valley reflect the Acadians' first farming endeavours; the long stretches of clear sand and sky against the vast ocean provide inspiration and respite for any weary traveller or local.

It is the intrinsic connection between land, sea and people that makes Nova Scotia's tremendous beauty all the more unique. Perhaps this is why it remains a coveted destination for visitors seeking natural splendour and a fine glass of wine, and for immigrants looking for fresh prospects and friendly communities to settle in. The wonders of Nova Scotia are many, and its roots remain authentic and strong.

ABOVE — In 1861 the discovery of gold in the hills near Sherbrooke Village instigated a gold rush. In more recent days, buildings from the traditional lumber and mining ways of life, like this old mill, have been restored.

BELOW — Scenic Cape Sable Island surrounded by only the sounds of the ocean waves crashing and the call of the occasional bird.

RIGHT ⌐ *Xavier Hall at St Francis Xavier University in Antigonish is the home of the university's Adult Education Program. The red brick building, which once encompassed all of St. FX, has been declared by the Historic Sites and Monuments Board of Canada a historic site. A commemorative plaque which hangs on the front of Xavier Hall reads:*

"Adverse economic conditions which led many to leave Eastern Nova Scotia in the early decades of this century gave rise to deep concern among staff of this university. Under the leadership of Fathers James Thompkins and Moses Coady, a program of self-help, based on American and European adult education ideas, was initiated. An Extension Department, formed in 1928, continues to work today, and students from around the world study the philosophy and methods of the Antigonish Movement at the Coady Institute on this campus."

PREVIOUS PAGE ⌐ *Nestled in the trees on a calm day, the millpond at the Balmoral Grist Mill creates a perfect mirror. Located southeast of Tatamagouche, the mill was built in 1874. Today, the water-powered mill is a fully restored living history museum, where visitors can see how flour was milled in the 1870s. Hiking trails and a picnic area overlook the pond. And yes, you can buy some of the milled flour for your own baking!*

Chester is a historic seaside village noted for a lively sailing history, beautiful summer homes, galleries and retail shops, and a relaxed lifestyle. From lush wildflowers to sparkling seascapes, Chester provides ample photo opportunities for its many visitors.

Red soil roads and expansive mud flats are characteristic of Economy, named after the Mi'kmaw word kenomee, meaning "a piece of land jutting out into the water." Located on the Minas Basin shore of the Bay of Fundy, Economy is a fabulous place to "walk on the bottom of the sea," when vast red sand flats are laid bare at low tide. Interpretive centres, hiking trails, and observation towers allow visitors to get close to the beauty of this geologically significant area.

Softly rounded hills of yellow and red interspersed with the dark green of fir and spruce follow the Margaree River as it meanders through the valley. Designated a Canadian Heritage River for its natural, cultural and historic values, the tranquil Margaree River is also well known for salmon fishing.

Grand-Pré's beautiful and pastoral landscape was once the Acadian homeland. It now exists as a National Historic Site and includes an interpretive centre that recounts the history of the Acadian people and their culture. After the deportation in 1755, the Acadians were scattered to many regions, but Grand-Pré remains in their hearts as a spiritual home.

ABOVE ⌒ *The fragility of an apple blossom on a tree in the Annapolis Valley. Vibrant colours—pink and red blossoms, green leaves, clear blue sky—are impossible to ignore in June in valley fields. The annual Apple Blossom Festival celebrates the beauty of the blossoms and the importance of the apple industry to the economy of the region.*

FACING PAGE ⌒ *The luscious apples of the Annapolis Valley, picked when they are perfectly ripe, exemplify the bounty of the valley and its horticultural history. Apples have been part of the province's trade with Europe and the United States for centuries. The marketplace continues to savour Nova Scotian grown apples—classic Spartans, Cortlands, and MacIntosh, and the newest varieties, Gala and Jonagold—which are regarded as some of the world's finest.*

With snow-covered fields surrounding its progress, the Gaspereau River provides a peaceful scene during the winter months. Come spring, it transforms into a prime recreational area with "tubing," swimming, and fishing—perfect ways to while away a lazy summer day.

ABOVE — *This nighttime view from Citadel Hill reflects the modern city, but also features the Town Clock, which arrived from England on June 10, 1803. The delivery of the clock was arranged by the Duke of Kent, younger son of George IV, who was sent to Nova Scotia to learn the art of governing. When he arrived, the duke was dismayed at the lack of discipline of the troops, who were consistently late for parade and duty. He had the timepiece installed so no one could claim they didn't know the time. With various upgrades in the building over the years, the timepiece itself is original, and is kept in perfect running order.*

FACING PAGE — *Lights sharply illuminate the towers and spires of St. Mary's Basilica against the dark night. Halifax is home to many Canadian firsts—for example, it is home to Canada's first Protestant church, St. Paul's, and its first basilica, St. Mary's. A Roman Catholic presence has been on this site since the first church, St. Peter's, was erected in 1782. St. Mary's Basilica replaced St. Peter's in 1820, and was consecrated on October 19, 1899. It is a National Historic Site.*

Reflecting the tranquility of the Gaspereau Valley near Wolfville, this idyllic scene of an old orchard and hay mower harks back to the early days of farming.

Rolling hills and working farms dot Cape Breton's landscape. Mabou, just over the crest of this farmer's field, is an area is known for its strong Scottish traditions. In fact, Gaelic is still taught in the local school, and in summer, the joyous sounds of Celtic music ring through the hills at ceilidhs (celebrations).

Peggy's Cove as seen from the land approaches over Cranberry Cove, during a very cold winter. The snow often doesn't stay long in this area of the province, buffeted as it is by winds, and often warmed by the ocean that surrounds it. In this case, cold air has frozen salt water that flowed over rocks at high tide, and then retreated, leaving ice pans and a hard glistening shell over the beloved rocks of the famous cove.

ABOVE ⌁ *Linking the year-round port of Halifax with the interior of the country, the railway was a vital part of Canada's growth. Still active today, the railway link cuts through residential areas of the peninsula of Halifax without any interruption of streets and sidewalks. The railway stands out in stark relief against the blanket of fresh snow, allowing us to focus on its enduring importance to the nation.*

FACING PAGE ⌁ *Scots Bay is located just past the spectacular look-off at Blomidon Provincial Park, before Cape Split. This sleepy picture of the seaside village offers just a glimpse of the long crescent beach, a rockhound's paradise. The area is popular with Annapolis Valley residents as a wonderful place to swim, and certainly a great place to hike and explore.*

ABOVE ⌐ *A tall ship is aglow at the Tall Ships Challenge hosted in Halifax in July of 2004. Once the new world's largest British enclave, Halifax has seen its share of tall ships, and the old port city continues to be a wonderful venue for these amazing vessels from all over the world. Renewed interest in tall ships keeps them travelling around the world, allowing people to see and touch a past that remains mysterious yet knowable.*

FACING PAGE ⌐ *The tall ship pictured is a ghostly reminder of days gone by, the harsh lights of night reflecting on its shrouds and decks.*

White sand and turquoise water invite bathers at Crystal Crescent Beach at East Pennant near Halifax. Even though the waters of Crystal Crescent are fully exposed to the open Atlantic and are frigid even in the summer, it is still a popular choice for beach lovers. Such pockets of sparkling white sand are treasures among the rocky shores of the granite coast, and the Provincial Park at the beach offers wonderful hiking and wildlife viewing.

The Cape d'Or lighthouse perches on a rocky finger of land that extends into the Minas Channel in the Bay of Fundy. The lighthouse is one of the most dramatically situated in the province, sitting in front of sheer cliffs that rise 150 metres behind it. Best of all, it is easily accessible, and the buildings that used to house the lightkeeper now serve as a restaurant and bed and breakfast.

BELOW ⌐ *Spiritual home of the Acadians, Grand-Pré National Park now exists as a memorial to the thousands who were forced to leave Nova Scotia starting in 1755. Beautiful gardens and an interpretative museum provide a destination for thousands of visitors each year.*

FACING PAGE ⌐ *A green jewel nestled in the rolling hills of a residential area of urban Halifax, the Ashburn Golf and Country Club has provided a welcome recreational pastime for members and guests since 1922. Designed by architect Stanley Thompson, Ashburn's old course offers the fine experience of playing traditional undulating fairways just minutes from the downtown core.*

OVERLEAF ⌐ *The rich colours of a setting sun pour over fishing boats in Indian Harbour. This fishing village lies on St Margaret's Bay, but is close to open ocean, and within five kilometres of the tourist destination Peggy's Cove. Boats still fish from the safety of coves like this all along Nova Scotia's coasts, even though the loss of fishing stock endangers centuries of tradition and livelihood. Even such hardships cannot lessen the impact of ocean, rocks and sunset in this homage to Nova Scotia and its inspiring beauty.*

ABOVE — *Also known as the "mini" Cabot Trail, the route from Malignant Cove to Ballantyne's Cove offers spectacular vistas of cliffs, ocean and valley. St. George's Bay is Nova Scotia's largest bay. This little village nestled among the hills looks to the sea for its livelihood, but is dependant on a large breakwater to keep its boats safe.*

FACING PAGE TOP — *Fishing boats rest dockside in the safe haven of Peggy's Cove on a frosty winter's day. A scenic destination for generations, this wintry scene is seldom seen by the majority of tourists who visit each year during the summer.*

FACING PAGE BOTTOM — *A warmer image of the famous Peggy's Cove, where boats are tied to stages in preparation for another fishing season. Despite the hundreds of thousands of tourists that arrive each summer to marvel at its scenic beauty, Peggy's Cove is very much a working community.*

ABOVE ⌐ A peaceful evening on the quiet waters of Lake Banook in Dartmouth. The lights welcome paddlers to Banook Canoe and Paddling Club, a Dartmouth Heritage Site and home of Canada's oldest rowing and paddling club. Lake Banook was part of the Mi'kmaw people's annual travel route from the Atlantic Ocean to the Bay of Fundy. In the late 1800s, entrepreneurs tried to commercialize this route by creating a series of locks and canals to connect shipping from the harbour to the Shubenacadie River, and in turn, to Minas Basin. Today, Lake Banook offers a world-class venue for paddling and rowing competitions, as well as a recreational area for swimming, boating, and winter skating.

FACING PAGE ⌐ These tide-ravaged timbers attest to the industry that existed along Advocate Bay in the Bay of Fundy. At one time, wharves enabled ships to be loaded with coal from inland deposits. Today the area is prized for its fossil cliffs and breathtaking scenery. In the distance is Isle Haute, first occupied by the French in their unsuccessful attempt to colonize the area.

ABOVE ⁓ *Cliffs of red and green along the Cabot Trail are sure to captivate with their amazing beauty, while the intense blue of the ocean hints at the danger that lurks beneath its surface. Our very own "Swiss Alps," the Cabot Trail offers an incredible variety of dazzling landscape and scenery.*

FACING PAGE ⁓ *From the vantage point of the Blomidon look-off, the fertile fields and orchards of the Annapolis Valley lay below like a patchwork quilt. Featured in the distance is the Minas Basin, home to myriad shipbuilders and traders of the past. On the way to Blomidon Provincial Park, the look-off is a perfect place to view Nova Scotia's close relationship with the sea.*

ABOVE ⁓ *This photo of simple but glorious water lilies emphasizes the diversity of habitat in Nova Scotia, a province with startling contrasts: from ocean to hillside, lakes to forests, and delicate pond flowers to crashing waves.*

FACING PAGE ⁓ *In June and early July, roadsides throughout Nova Scotia are often filled with the variegated colours of the lupin (Lupinus perennis). These hardy flowers are nitrogen-fixers, thereby mitigating the effects of winter road salt in the soil, as well as offering great beauty.*

ABOVE ⌒ *The Cabot Trail in Cape Breton offers wonderful opportunities to see the coastline. Burnished by a setting sun, this rock-strewn inlet reflects the peacefulness so many come here to enjoy.*

FACING PAGE ⌒ *Eastern Passage gained notoriety during the American Revolution when ships carrying contraband used it to bypass the batteries at Point Pleasant Park.*

Fishing boats, mooring buoys, and a tranquil ocean with the sun just appearing frame this view of Lunenburg Bay at Blue Rocks. A small village that makes its living from the sea, Blue Rocks has become a vacation destination for many. With its rock-strewn vistas and ocean vantage point, it epitomizes classic Nova Scotian beauty.

ABOVE ⁓ *Sharp shadows and a curving river provide a fine portrait of winter's beauty in one of Nova Scotia's most beautiful regions. The Cornwallis River meanders from the heart of the Annapolis Valley to the tidal shores of the Minas Basin. Its journey epitomizes the diversity of the province, as it travels from rich agricultural farms to the sea.*

FACING PAGE ⁓ *This scene of the Dingle Tower in winter is another example of the many recreational areas that exist along Halifax's waterways. Located in Sir Sandford Fleming Park, the tower was built in 1916 to commemorate the first elected assembly in the British Empire, which was convened in Halifax on October 2, 1758. The park was named after the donor, Sir Sandford Fleming, the creator of Universal Standard Time, designer of the first adhesive Canadian postage stamp, and engineer of the Canadian Pacific Railway. The tower is named after Sir Sandford's summer home, which was known as the Dingle.*

ABOVE — *Wild rose bushes and lupins provide a colourful foreground to a pretty scene of boats resting at low tide at the harbour in Advocate, perhaps stealing a quiet moment during a busy workday.*

FACING PAGE — *During July 2004, Halifax was host to the international Tall Ships Challenge. In this scene, reminiscent of an artists' canvas from the past, the tall ships proceed along the harbourfront and then out to sea, racing to be the first, or just to finish another demanding leg of the Challenge.*

OVERLEAF — *Sunrise on Ingonish Beach. Though in this image the sand and sea are isolated, they won't remain so for long. The beach is located just outside the Cape Breton Highlands National Park and is a popular tourist destination. The two large bays which make up Ingonish are separated by the ruggedly beautiful Middle Head Peninsula. Ingonish has breathtaking scenery, and numerous outdoor recreational activities including hiking, deep-sea fishing, whale watching, bicycling, sea kayaking, and skiing.*

BELOW — *Schooner races skirt the downtown shoreline of Halifax and Dartmouth. The capital region of the province is graced with a harbour accessible year-round. The considerable size and depth of the harbour means it can accommodate the largest sea-going cargo ships in the world, but it still offers recreational opportunities for more casual boating enthusiasts.*

FACING PAGE — *Bluenose II moves north along the harbour in Halifax under a perfect summer sky. This is Nova Scotia's floating ambassador, a tribute to generations of skilled Nova Scotians. Built by a beer merchant, Bluenose II was meant to commemorate the original and was crafted in the same manner, and at the same boat yard, as its namesake. The schooner is owned by a public trust and travels to other ports to promote the province, as well as offering sailing tours in summer months.*

At Rocky Bay, off the Cabot Trail, the blues of the ocean shimmer beneath the wide summer sky. At the edge of the bay, a few fishing boats bob against the dock. Such an idyllic scene captures the heart of Nova Scotia's deep ties to the sea.

Another peaceful spot in Nova Scotia is found at Lower Prospect. The community was built around this safe haven for fishing boats and was well protected from the ravages of the North Atlantic. Most of today's residents do not fish, but are appreciative of this enticing view.

ABOVE ⁓ *Autumn colours emphasize the unique beauty of Victoria Park in Truro. The park has over a hundred acres of trees, featuring ancient hemlocks that tower above a steep chasm, as well as a stream and two waterfalls. Victoria Park also has a replica of the Holy Well, an Acadian baptismal site of the seventeenth and eighteenth centuries.*

FACING PAGE ⁓ *Bealach Ban Falls in Cape Breton offers all waterfall enthusiasts an opportunity to marvel at these natural wonders. These falls provide real steps up a gorge—Bealach is Gaelic for "pass," indicating they must have been used as a route through rough terrain for the area's first settlers. Today, they provide a place ideal for quiet, restful contemplation.*

OVERLEAF ⁓ *Starkly outlined by a rich sunset, jagged rock formations attest to the ferocity of tide and wind. Now part of the Blomidon Provincial Park, Cape Split is accessed by a hiking trail that offers magnificent views across the Minas Channel to Cape d'Or and Advocate Harbour.*

ABOVE ⌐ *Swans in the winter snow at the Public Gardens brave the icy pond. Although the gardens are closed to human visitors in winter, the ducks, geese, and swans enjoy the peace and quiet of such a pastoral spot in the midst of busy Halifax.*

FACING PAGE ⌐ *This serene and almost mystical image of the bandstand in the Public Gardens in Halifax illustrates that this jewel of a park is indeed a superb example of urban green space. Built originally in 1887, and refurbished many times, the bandstand was integral to the Victorian image of a public garden with seating for concert goers, a maze of pathways, and miniature bridges for romantic strolls. This is all set amidst an abundance of greenery, as shrubs, trees, flowers, and statues complete the scene from a bygone era.*

ABOVE — *Perched atop the prominent Gallows Hill stands the Lunenburg Academy, at the UNESCO World Heritage Site of Lunenburg. A public school in the tradition of the "acadamies" that dot the province, the Lunenburg Academy was built in 1894 and completed in 1895. With a distinctive red roof that can be seen for miles, the school is maintained as a learning institution.*

FACING PAGE — *The bold reds and yellows of autumn leaves are reflected in the tranquil waters of one of Kejimkujik National Park's myriad lakes. Located in the south of the province, "Keji," as it is affectionately known, is one of the most visited parks in Canada's park system. Home to native petroglyphs and ancient hemlock forests, the park is an all-season wilderness refuge of great scenic beauty, as well as being home to the only extant population of Blanding's turtles in Canada.*

ABOVE ⟋ *The fusion of sand, sea, and sky are a head-turning combination in this incredible image of Inverness Beach and village along the Cabot Trail. The village itself is home to the Inverness Miner's Museum, which highlights the region's coal-mining history. An extensive boardwalk along the beach allows walkers to soak in the beauty of the area.*

FACING PAGE ⟋ *Nova Scotia's Eastern shore is treasured for its many white sand beaches. Clam Harbour Beach, home of the annual Sand Castle Sculpture Festival, is a coveted destination for beach enthusiasts at all times of the year.*

ABOVE ⟶ *Salt spray churns off the tops of swirling waves at Chebucto Head. Still visible are the bare bones of coastal defences and fortifications built during World War II to protect the approaches to Halifax Harbour. The harbour was vital for the war effort due to its size and all-year accessibility—convoys of ships congregated there to take soldiers and vital supplies to England. Chebucto Head today is a popular viewing point for seals, whales, and ships.*

FACING PAGE ⟶ *Fishing boats line up in Digby Harbour. Here, the Digby scallop fleet—the largest fleet in the province—awaits the season. Bristling with lines and technology, the boats seem ready to march away.*

The beauty of autumn leaves adds another season of opportunity for visiting Mary Ann Falls, which is a haven in summer for swimmers and sunbathers. In winter, the area becomes popular with skiers. There are many such waterfalls in the Highlands, but not all are as easily accessed, making these waterfalls the most visited.

ABOVE ⁓ *Ocean meets sky and land at a small beach in LaHave. The coastal tides promote the growth of rockweed, a common seaweed found on beaches in Nova Scotia. Rockweed used to be harvested with the help of oxen, and spread onto fields as a fertilizer.*

FACING PAGE ⁓ *The broad expanse of the LaHave River reflects the cloudy sky, in this photo taken looking downriver toward the Riverport area. A traveller can enjoy much of LaHave River's scenic beauty on roads that run parallel to its shores.*

This view of the North West Arm looks out towards the harbour approaches, one of the scenic wonders of the Halifax urban landscape. The Dingle Tower stands in the distance, behind the many recreational boats at anchor and mooring. The Arm is a recreational treasure, boasting two yacht clubs, numerous private clubs, estates, and residences on its shores.

ABOVE — *The resort at White Point Beach is shrouded in misty sunlight as waves brush the shore. A private one-kilometre-long beach allows guests at the resort to enjoy the sand and waves. It also provides a haven for the birds that use the shoreline for their food and home.*

FACING PAGE — *In winter there are many scenes along Nova Scotia's highways that are reminiscent of a northern landscape. This "no man's land" is located on highway 103, along the south shore. Beautiful but inhospitable, such an eerie scene is tinged with the supernatural.*

ABOVE — *The sweeping vista of Lawrencetown Beach on Nova Scotia's eastern shore. For many years, this beach has been a home to Nova Scotia surfers, as its huge waves from the north Atlantic beckon these hardy souls to test their mettle. The large house on the horizon is MacDonald House, once a family home, and now a museum, gift shop, and tea shop.*

FACING PAGE — *Lunenburg, a UNESCO World Heritage Site, as seen from across the harbour. Lunenburg is a colourful and captivating town that radiates its seafaring heritage. The red buildings on the shoreline are the Fisheries Museum of the Atlantic, a complex devoted to the history of commercial fishing in Maritime Canada. The town also boasts a foundry, a marine blacksmith, and a dory shop that opened in 1895 and still builds traditional dories. The historic buildings honoured by UNESCO now house inns, restaurants, shops galleries and residences.*

Likely the three most photographed churches in Canada, these landmarks are in the picturesque village of Mahone Bay. A host of small retail shops, dining and recreational opportunities, and a quiet charm help define this coastal gem.

ABOVE ⌐ *Nicknamed "Nova Scotia's masterpiece," the Cabot Trail on Cape Breton Island features many breathtaking vistas. The beach at Black Brook is a favourite spot for those who enjoy rugged landscapes and the natural beauty of rock, ocean and sky. The small beach, cut in two by Black Brook, is embraced by a headland on one side. Like Ingonish Beach, the sand is washed away each winter and redeposited each spring! Over the course of the year, the sandspit at the mouth of the brook shifts continuously, dependent on the tides and currents.*

FACING PAGE ⌐ *In Herring Cove, just along the approaches to Halifax Harbour, fishing boats, fish stores, and stages, as well as recreational boats, congregate in a finger-shaped cove that offers safe anchorage from rough seas and storms. Long celebrated for its incredible beauty, Herring Cove is a popular home base for downtown workers seeking tranquility after a busy workday in Halifax.*

OVERLEAF ⌐ *Water recedes as waves begin their renewed assault on a rocky beach at the foot of soaring cliffs. The coastal trail on the Cabot Trail is remarkable for such sights and remains a beacon for those who love to explore such hidden pockets of beauty.*

The Halifax waterfront's boardwalk on a crisp winter morning is quiet and
peaceful, as the outline of ships tied up at the Maritime Museum of the Atlantic
provides echoes of days gone by. These permanent reminders of Nova Scotia's
sea-going past are also tributes to the people who served on them, even
throughout long, fierce winters.

ABOVE ⌒ *The setting sun casts a warm light as the ocean breakers prepare to launch against a rocky beach on the Cabot Trail. Continually changing and always entrancing, such scenes provide lasting memories for residents and visitors.*

OVERLEAF ⌒ *A makeshift footbridge across the Gaspereau River provides access to fields, allowing a farmer to cross the river with cattle each day to lead them to grazing pastures. Such a bridge might also lend easy entry to a favourite rafting spot for landowners along the riverbank, or be an added convenience in spring, when rushing high water prevents crossing at other sites.*

Viewed from sandy Hirtle's Beach, unceasing ocean waves wash the sand, enticing all to walk and play.

The farming community of Milford, just outside Truro, is known for its dairy products. Such farms are common in an area that contributes so much to the quality of life in Nova Scotia. The province's roots in the land are as strong as its ties to the sea.

ABOVE ⌐ *With the continual flushing of the tides, the ocean deposits wonderful treasures for beachcombers, ranging from rounded pieces of coloured glass to silky-smooth driftwood. This large piece of driftwood, washed up on a quiet shore in Parrsborro, offers a peaceful natural seat on which to observe a golden sunset.*

FACING PAGE ⌐ *Three Fathom Harbour at sunrise. Graceful, long-legged herons make an appearance while searching the muddy coasts for food.*

ABOVE ⁓ *Against a stunning backdrop of rich autumn reds and golds, a horse grazes contently in a roadside field near Amherst. Such an image, which recalls older days, manages to endure into the twenty-first century.*

FACING PAGE ⁓ *Lush red apples cluster on trees in the Annapolis Valley between Digby and Middleton. Autumn in the valley provides a bountiful array of apples, as well as delicious and abundant harvest vegetables such as squash, pumpkins, and peppers, causing local farmers' markets and roadside stands to become vibrant with colour.*

ABOVE — *A rainbow over Margaree Harbour offers more good luck in its mystical arc as it hovers over the protected inner harbour of the colourful coastal village. The sand beaches provide perfect vantage points for watching crashing waves and bounding surf.*

FACING PAGE — *Gentle waves lap the sand at Crescent Beach. The smooth sand beach offers a wonderful opportunity for walking, sunning, and enjoying the expansive sky. The beach extends along the roadway to the LaHave Islands, a delightful microcosm of "old time" Nova Scotia.*

ABOVE — *Cape George, with a view of the ocean-worn cliffs in the background. The Cape George Heritage Trails provide a fantastic hiking experience, with over thirty kilometres of trails that offer ocean views and coastline walking. Even better, hot and tired hikers can take a relaxing dip in the ocean afterwards.*

FACING PAGE — *A winding dirt road leads the way to Brier Island in Digby County, along the Evangeline Trail. This picturesque island, though only four miles long, is a popular destination for locals and tourists alike. Whale-watching, hiking, and viewing some of the world's highest tides are a draw for visitors from around the world.*

OVERLEAF — *The unique design of the Yarmouth lighthouse is a rare sight. The lighthouse, which has a narrower base than top, sits about forty metres above sea level. Lighthouses still keep watch over the waves of the Atlantic, providing valuable safety beacons to ships.*